Cucumber

Helping children to know and love their vegetables

Carmel Houston-Price, Bethany Chapman, Katrina Dulay, Natalie Ellison, Kate Harvey, Natalie Masento and David Messer

Published by the University of Reading, Reading, UK
Copyright © University of Reading

ISBN: 978-0-7049160-4-3

All rights reserved. No part of this book may be reproduced or transmitted in any form or by any means, electronic or mechanical, including photocopying, recording, or by any information storage and retrieval system, without permission in writing from the publisher.

SEE & EAT is a trademark.

Design by Fuzzy Flamingo
www.fuzzyflamingo.co.uk

Images used under license from Shutterstock.com

The story of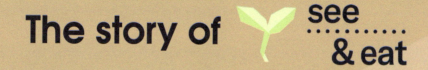

The SEE & EAT team are passionate about helping little ones to know and love their vegetables!

We know it can be difficult for parents to persuade young children to eat a variety of vegetables and we have been working hard on ways to make this easier. Research led by Professor Carmel Houston-Price at the University of Reading has shown that pre-schoolers are more likely to eat vegetables at mealtimes if they are already familiar with how the vegetable looks and where it comes from. The more familiar your child is with a food before it appears on their plate, the better… and this is especially true for vegetables they don't like or haven't tried before!

SEE & EAT books are an easy, effective and fun way to introduce children to vegetables before they try them.

SEE & EAT books help children to get to know their vegetables by showing each food's journey 'from farm to fork'. Our research shows that looking at a SEE & EAT picture book with your child for a few minutes each day for a couple of weeks is enough to make a difference. After looking at one of our books, children are often more willing to taste the vegetable than they were beforehand. They eat more of it, and seem to enjoy eating it more, too!

For more information about the research behind SEE & EAT, visit our website at www.research.reading.ac.uk/kids-food-choices

How to use this book to help your little one to know and love cucumber!

- Look at this book about cucumber with your child for a few minutes every day for a couple of weeks.
- Make reading time fun! Find a time and place to look at the cucumber book each day that works best for you and your child. Feel free to look at the book in your own way. You might want to talk about whether you have ever grown or picked cucumbers yourself, where you usually buy cucumbers, or how you like to prepare and eat them. Always be positive about cucumbers!
- After two weeks, go shopping for a cucumber with your child, if you can. Point them out in the shop and involve your child in preparing the cucumber back at home. You might want to try our simple recipes at the end of this book. Then, serve it up. It's time to find out whether your child will crunch on their cucumber!
- Remember to chop vegetables into small pieces and to keep an eye on your little ones while they are eating, especially if they are just starting to eat solid foods or the vegetable is new to them.
- Even if they taste just a single slice, that is a great start. Don't worry if they refuse to eat it, keep on offering cucumber at mealtimes and they are likely to accept it in the end.
- Then it's time to choose another of our vegetable books so that your little one can learn to love another vegetable!

These are cucumbers. Look at how long and green they are!

Cucumbers can be long or short and their skin can be smooth or bumpy. Some are even a bit prickly!

Cucumbers grow in a field like this one, when the weather is warm and sunny, or in a greenhouse.

These cucumbers are big and firm enough to pick.

How many cucumbers can you see? Some of them are hiding!

Time to cut the cucumber from the plant!

We usually buy a whole cucumber but sometimes you can buy half a cucumber.

You can cut a cucumber into round pieces...

… or into long sticks.

We usually eat it raw, without cooking it.

It is tasty with a dip…

… or in a salad.

Which other vegetables can you see in this salad?

Did you know that you can puree cucumber to make a cold soup?

More ideas to help your child to know and love their vegetables!

- Could you grow your own cucumbers? Cucumbers grow well in a pot on the windowsill or in a sunny spot in the garden.
- Take your child to a farm shop or farmer's market or look out for open days at local farms.
- In the supermarket, let your child find and choose a cucumber for you, and point out their different shapes and sizes.
- Encourage your child to explore the look, smell and feel of a cucumber by hiding one in a bag alongside other vegetables and playing a guessing game to see if your child can identify them by touch, smell or hearing you describe them.
- Let your child be your little helper in the kitchen. Choose a simple recipe and talk through the steps. Children can help wash the vegetables, put ingredients in a bowl or pass you utensils.
- Try to ensure that vegetables cover one third of their plate so that your child learns what a healthy meal looks like.
- And remember… it is a good idea to eat together as a family if you can, even if this is just one meal at the weekend. It could be at breakfast, lunch or dinnertime – whatever works best for your family.
- Visit our website (www.seeandeat.org) for more activities and games and to download SEE & EAT ebooks.

Simple suggestions for preparing cucumber

Simple green salad

1. Cut a cucumber into thin slices.
2. Add the slices of cucumber to a bowl with pieces of tomato and lettuce leaves.

Cucumber soup

1. Chop a cucumber into thin slices and place these in a saucepan with a little vegetable stock and some mint leaves.
2. Simmer for about 15 minutes.
3. Add a little Greek yogurt and use a blender to puree the soup until it is smooth.
4. Chill in the fridge and serve cold.

We would love to hear how you get on with the
SEE & EAT books and activities.

Share your stories with us by emailing us at
SeeAndEat@reading.ac.uk

or by contacting the project lead,
Professor Carmel Houston-Price
School of Psychology & Clinical Language Sciences,
University of Reading,
Earley Gate,
Whiteknights,
Reading, UK
RG6 6ES

Acknowledgements

The SEE & EAT team at the University of Reading are indebted to the hundreds of children, parents, teachers and healthcare professionals who have taken part in the research studies, workshops and focus groups that have helped us make SEE & EAT activities as effective as they can be.

We are grateful to EIT Food for funding the work of the SEE & EAT team since 2019. EIT Food is the innovation community for Food of the European Institute of Innovation and Technology (EIT), a body of the EU under Horizon 2020, the EU Framework Programme for Research and Innovation.

We are also grateful to our partners at the Open University, the Universities of Turin, Warsaw and Helsinki, British Nutrition Foundation (BNF) and the European Food Information Council (EUFIC), who have helped to bring SEE & EAT activities to families across Europe.

Finally, we would like to thank Jen Parker at Fuzzy Flamingo (www.fuzzyflamingo.co.uk) for her support with the design and publication of this series of books and Sascha Landskron at Boom House Books (www.boomhousebooks.co.uk) for her enthusiasm for the SEE & EAT project, and for her support with marketing and promotion.

– Professor Carmel Houston-Price & the SEE & EAT team (Dr Bethany Chapman, Lily Clark, Dr Katrina May Dulay, Natalie Ellison, Professor Kate Harvey, Dr Sun Ae Kim, Dr Natalie Masento, Professor David Messer, Dr Alan Roberts)

Look out for the other books in the SEE & EAT series ...

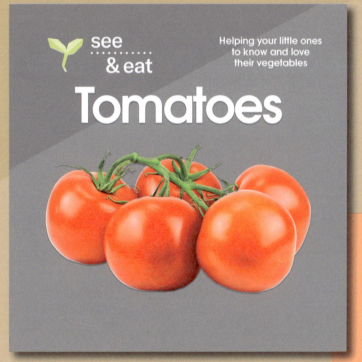

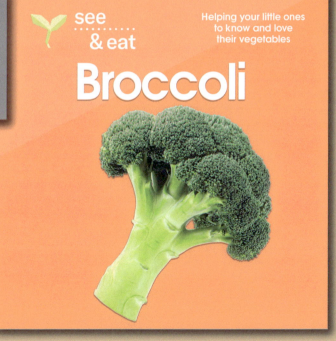

… and many more. Visit www.seeandeat.org for the library of ebooks and printed books that are now available in this series.